A B C
FOR THE

LIBRARY

story and pictures by Mary E. Little

ATHENEUM 1975 NEW YORK

Library of Congress Cataloging in Publication Data
Little, Mary E
    ABC for the library.
    SUMMARY: An alphabetical introduction to the
library using such realities as desk and globe and such
abstract concepts as joy and knowledge.
    1. Libraries—Juvenile literature.   [1. Alphabet
books.   2. Libraries]   I. Title.
Z665.5.L58   027.62'5   75-6825
ISBN 0-689-30467-6

Copyright © 1975 by Mary E. Little
All rights reserved
Published simultaneously in Canada by
McClelland & Stewart, Ltd.
Manufactured in the United States of America
Printed by Connecticut Printers, Hartford, Connecticut
Bound by A. Horowitz and Son / Bookbinders,
Clifton, New Jersey
First Edition

To the children—

all of them

A

is for
this **ABC**

and **a**ll the fun in the library.

B is for **B**ooks and **b**orrowing.

You can read about everything.

C is for your library Card.

Just sign your name; that's not so hard.

D is for

Desk.

That is where

you check books out—

and return them there.

E is for **E**asy, the books you need

when you begin to learn to read.

F is for **F**ilm

and **F**airy tale

and Friday at four o'clock

without fail.

G is for **G**lobe
and **g**eography;

H is for **H**eroes and **h**istory.

I is for *I*s.

Where would we be without **i**t **i**n an ABC?

J is for Jingle and
Joke and joy and
jolly riddles for girl or boy.

K is for **K**itten and famous **K**ings and **k**nowledge: **k**nowing about such things.

STORY HOUR

JAN. 6, 4 P.M.

L is for Library, Listen and Look.

There's lots of fun inside a book.

M is for **M**agic and **M**other Goose.

N is for **N**ature books, **n**ovels

and **n**ews.

is for **O**ut.

The book for you

has been taken **O**ut—

and is **O**ver-due!

P

is for Puppet-show,

Picture-book, and

Peep-show, too.

Come, have a look.

Q is for **Q**uestion: what's a **q**uery?

Look the word up in the

dictionary.

R is for **R**ead

and **r**ead

and **r**ead

and

Reference books

big children need.

S is for **S**tories,
to hear, to read,
and **S**ongs to **S**ing,
and **S**igns to heed.

?

Ask the Librarian

T is for **T**itle,
Text,
and **T**ale;

for books **t**hat **t**alk

and **T**ales in Braille.

 is for the **U**niverse.

Books will help you **U**nderstand.

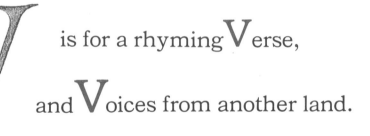 is for a rhyming **V**erse,

and **V**oices from another land.

We **W**onder **W**hether **W**e **W**ere **W**rong about the **W**eather.

is the hardest letter, I guess,

to make an ABC eXpress…

Y is for **Y**ou and **Y**ou

and and **Y**ou and

You

and You

and even

You...

Z is for **Z**ip
and **Z**est and
Zoom.

Come again to the children's room!